Beliefs considered spiritually

Katja Kubiak

- Recognize beliefs.
- Beliefs, what is it?
- what are negative beliefs?
- where do they come from and what does that mean?
- How much debt do parents have?

dissolve negative beliefs and overlay or exchange them through positive beliefs?

- Which way is the best?
- the observer in us (inner observer)

the talking part of our consciousness,

Activate it and let it have its say

- get to know the inner critic briefly
- Beliefs regarding the treatment of our children
- the most beautiful affirmations for children and parents

Good morning

Since we are confronted and raised in childhood with sometimes hair-raising beliefs, here is a small precaution.

That our children will not have the same problems as us later on.

And to which we ourselves also

believe in us again, trust us and are no longer dependent on others who always think they know everything better.

First, an explanation of the terms.

What are beliefs?

Beliefs in themselves are all that we carry around with us in our heads every day.

That which is the first thought that flows through our minds when we face a situation.

That's what sometimes preoccupies us over hours, other people over years or even their whole lives.

Most beliefs are subconscious and don't really come to light.

Most of our words, deeds, and actions are actually based on what we have learned. On our beliefs.

Knowing this alone, however, is far from sufficient.

Who wants or should change must begin to question. He has to question himself, listen to himself and hear WHAT comes out.

There are many ways to do this, but first let's examine the beliefs.

We generally distinguish all unconscious beliefs into negative and positive. Since most of humanity now has more problems with the negative part, we begin with it.

Negative beliefs

What is that?

Negative beliefs are all that slows us down, makes us afraid, robs energy, inhibits our complete growth, slows down our progress, and never makes us grow to true greatness.

They are negative opinions, thoughts, prejudices, negative experiences whose bad results have become entrenched in us, sucked in. We just can't overcome or get rid of.

Which we have either brought into this world from our previous incarnations, but which are very often taught to us from birth by our parents and relatives.

They keep pulling us down, which prevent us from going into the day in a positive mood. They often do not show us a positive light from life and our future.

Not to mention that this is already going on in kindergarten and school and that we and our children are almost always only reminded of the mistakes. Or why are there grades and ratings, but only to make it clear "here you are bad".

Negative thoughts and beliefs manifest themselves even if one is constantly criticized, is often questioned, and is never or rarely praised and built up.

Pay attention to your words and communicate empathetic, positively with yourself and with others. Is the first piece of advice to be given to yourself all the time.

Where do negative beliefs actually come from?

I would like to share my own thoughts.

Children still come into the world like raw diamonds, and pretty much everyone thinks they're adding their mustard, and the more often this happens, the more erroneous, estimating, derisive thoughts and feelings are engraved.

When the child grows up, he carries all this ballast with him all the time. This is also one reason why we become more and more bitter,gritty and bitter over the years.

Or how often do they still see with all their hearts, happy laughing adults??

How often do you have adults dancing in the rain and jumping through puddles, conjuring snow angels in the snow, walking across a flower meadow in amazement?

Staring at the moon and I'm looking forward to a ladybug?

When was the last time they sang cheerfully and wrongly loudly and laughed at each other with their friends?

Let's face it, the majority of our adults are almost dead inside. Children have to be calm and quiet, then they are good.

As soon as they laugh and sing, they say "give rest."

Romp outside and play football on the meadow. How often is this forbidden?

How often have residents simply hated the playground next door and protested against it.

In Leipzig, the city I am from, there was even an unsightly contemporary who shot at the children playing in the playground with bow and arrow.

Just as these negative guys like to poison dogs, some people don't shy away from hurting people.

These people are full, up to the top with negative thoughts and beliefs. They have no heart for the children or even for animals and other adults on the outside.

Still for her inner child. They have often simply forgotten this.

So where does this come about?

How did it came about?

Where and when do negative beliefs form?

As with all other things, it can have many reasons.

Often it is the reason that in the course of one has experienced so many setbacks, disappointments, betrayal and slander, lies and frauds,

that it is better to close one's way to everyone.

It is almost safer to lock yourself up, not to trust others at all and to leave no one to go.

When you sit in your inner bunker and wait for death or just wait for everything to get better on its own, everything that would bring light and love is really not needed.

Unfortunately, when people are waiting for everything to improve on their own, they are usually unlucky.

For it is not for nothing that it is called "nothing comes from nothing".

In fact, it is also a belief, but rather in the category of motivation.

Unfortunately, one of the beliefs that most of humanity does not want to believe. Many people suddenly find it all "quite okay" when they realize that change must always begin in them. Or they are still so firmly in their comfort zone that change is not feasible without a new mindset – a kind of reprogramming of their thinking.

Now that they have read so far, I assume that they do not belong to this genus of human beings, that they want to make more of themselves and their lives, and that they above all want to welcome light and love into their lives.

I am pleased about that!

How many times have I cursed inwardly when I meet these kind of people for whom everything is too much?

Those who are not interested in others. They are always only concerned with their own advantage and others are just annoying with their kind.

Who needs Miesepeter around him? They shout out their negative beliefs loudly and again and again into the world until our ears almost bleed.

We should be aware, however, that the majority of these miesepeters can do nothing about it. These people are a product of their environment and often the circumstances that led to this behaviour are more than tragic.

It is also tragic, however, that many of them are not yet helping, as mentioned above, do not want to or cannot be helped.

There is the aspect in reincarnation theory that we come to earth to grow spiritually and emotionally

and often it is the young souls who simply do not have this growth in this life.

The souls still at the very beginning of their incarnation cycle. Who want to get to know all aspects of being human and need to know first?

These are particularly receptive to all that is somehow getting on the nerves of old souls.

Their behavior is often very much to the chagrin of the old or older souls, who would like to help and cannot or may not.

When you meet such souls/people, you should just realize that it is so good for them and you cannot do much now.

Not every man on this earth must attain enlightenment in this life. Just as not every man has any precincing to heaven after his death.

These people often carry their negative beliefs around like a cup.

And we are already on the subject:

How much guilt do parents have?

Spiritually, truly little! We are already born as a soul or with our soul. And there are many thoughts and entanglements to our earlier lives already present.

We have chosen where we want to be born. What we want to learn in the world in this life.

Our parents are more likely to be tools for our spiritual growth. You are chosen to be our parents. There are no coincidences.

Our parents must cope with our "god-given character" from birth. Those who have children know full well that every single child is different from birth. Especially in character.

It is funny, if you look at it, that everyone should be the same purely biologically, because we all come into the world with the same conditions.

So, there must be more before the start.

Very few people I know even think about it. I do, and that's why I initiate them into my own thoughts.

Do they want examples of negative beliefs now?

This list would suddenly expand the book by a hundred pages. That is why I'm looking for the ones that probably every one of us has heard before and hates inwardly.

- life is not a pony farm
- I grow up first and then we see more
- if you stretch your feet under my table, I have to say thishere
- what do you think you are?
- you think we all need to listen to you

- come to my age...

is this enough for the beginning? It's even harder.

- Do not be so foolish
- Do not always be so whining
- shame yourself
- you make me ready, crazy, insane
  that stressed me animalically
- I do not pack that anyway
- I can no longer help
- I am not worth it anyway
- no one loves me

You can see, this list can really fill books. Especially since each of us has almost 8 billion people of our own beliefs and carries them with us.

These thoughts are the ballast that our environment has charged us over the years. In addition to what we have already brought with us.

Wouldn't it be nice to be completely free of these literally sick and sick thoughts?

Related to be able to convert these thoughts into positive energy and power?

Beliefs regarding how to deal with our children

Positive beliefs, i.e. affirmations, should always be applied when we notice, for example:

- Stop, our child is talking something negative.

- I just told my child nonsense.

- I have just really offended, hurt, wronged someone by saying something that comes from my own thinking, but that does not affect him at all.

-My expectations towards a person or thing are completely wrong. Oh, what did I actuallysay??

First aid in this case would be:

We take the negative things and transform them into positive things. We are just trying to bend what we have just done. Hoping that the damage is not too great.

Whether that works is another matter and for the most part is also related to whether we are seriously ashamed and apologetic when we have said crap or built it. Or whether we talk badly to ourselves again.

When we say negative things to children, it is always bad. Children are by themselves honest journeymen who are entitled to be confronted with them always and everywhere appreciatively and lovingly

Just as it is said that one has to tell a child about 1000 times in order to remember this, many of us now have to tell our child the positive beliefs 1000 times, so that many negative things that we have told them are eradicated.

Each of us probably knows what we say so negatively to our children, so I can save myself the enumerae.

Most of them are probably already listed above.

When I say that thoughts and words have to be said around 1000 times before they are properly internalized, one has to admit that it could be very difficult to get rid of or transform really negative thoughts in the reverse-art.

Above all, who please will stick to it and tell himself 1000 times? At least I do not.

How did I manage to erase most of the negative things from my brain? We will then add to this.

Let us catch ourselves by wanting to make other adults feel evil or to put our beliefs on their eyes,

Then it is often the case that we ourselves either still firmly believe in the nonsense that we have been told, or we do not want ours to change for the better, or even to become better than ourselves.

We ourselves also sit quite often in a kind of comfort zone and the many nonsensical beliefs prevent us from actively growing.

But first, how do I prevent me from putting negative beliefs in my child's head?

Here is a small example:

They catch themselves, during their child's often rather tough homework checks; to say the following:

"oh man, I've told you a thousand times, you never become anything because you're just too messy and lazy."

Ooh, that sat. Our child hears, "You will never become anything, for you are too stupid."

This negative belief is imprinted much faster than you probably imagine.

They do not have to pronounce it 1000 times and hang relatively quickly, in the subconscious of their child.

Still as a reminder:

If their parents used to talk to them like this, they are no longer surprised if they still think they have made nothing of their lives. Or nothing to be worth and so on.

These thoughts, they owe to their parents. Or others who have met them so much. They have already learned that. Our parents have a little guilt ;)

If they now also notice, their inner child becomes very sadly in sync with their own child,

then they simply take the positive beliefs at their hand and overlay them over the old, negative scrap sentences.

You can and should train, so that you don't say so many bad things in advance.

My first method:

Let their inner voice speak again.

Resuscitation their inner observer.

What is the inner observer? How can I resuscitation it?

The inner observer is such a mix of our reason and our consciousness. He is our inner voice. He always looks at what we are doing and can look critically at it. But it can also help to change situations.

The inner observer knows what is right andr wrong and determines when we make mistakes, which we sometimes make through our ego or also carry out again and again through old, negative beliefs.

It is he who helps us to leave our negative path and to try to become positive.

But as I said, you must make it consciously activate and work. In the beginning, he will not speak to us. But we can ask him to do so.

If, of course, he speaks to us and we don't want to hear it and just ignore it, then there will be little change to the positive.

To the inner observer there is already a lot to read in the spiritual literature and somehow everyone has such a slightly modified opinion. There are several aspects of our soul.

Our soul also consists of many different parts. The inner observer is one of them.

Few people know all aspects of the soul and this should not be an issue in this book.

In addition to the inner observer, there is also the inner critic that is the one who cries the loudest.

And probably also the one who carries all the beliefs with him.

It must be turned quieter. From him speaks the voice of reason, which is instilled in our hands from the outside.

The inner critic wants us to adapt to everything, not to notice. Speak obedient and inconspicuous living.

When we did mischief as a child, he took over the voice of our parents and made us feel bad.

Of course, there are also people in whom the inner critic has been mercilessly silenced. Those who ignore all caution, who know no grace and no fear.

Every part of our soul has a task and a raison d'etre. It is only necessary to reassignits place to eachshare.

The inner critic then becomes someone who only gives us proposals but no longer constantly puts us in the way if we do not act according to his will.

The inner observer then becomes someone who takes care of our actions and ensures that we are truly valuable to ourselves and to others. And treat us and our environment with respect.

In this way, we also learn to question each of our thoughts. Looking behind the facade and recognizing:

Is this idea negative?

"Does this thought benefit me or does it slow me down?

"Do I really need this idea?

"Isn't it time to let go of this thought?

"How much better is it without this thought?

"How much better is my environment if I give up this idea?

small exercise:

If a stupid sentence is already out there and they notice it immediately, then honest remorse and withdrawal can make a big difference!

Children are well aware of whether they mean it honestly. or not.

If they are far too sour on themselves or others now, then they take a short break, count up to 10 or breathe through 3 times deeply.

If they already suspect that a situation could escalate, then please, do they get used to strategies beforehand to defuse this situation in advance or not to let it arise in the first place.

If it is unavoidable, they practice the different versions of their behavior on their own.

It also takes a lot of pressure out of one, if you already know how to react adequately in various unpleasant situations.

Ask yourself the above questions.

Play them to themselves and theirs and paint positive versions of situational processes, also how they can react at what moment.

So that they learn to stay relaxed and cool in the long run.

Often you go into different situations with negative thoughts and you suggest being negative towards you.

Our environment only reflects us. If we are positive and minded, our environment will also be positive.

A change in the basic attitude to the positive can also contribute to the much looser and more relaxed ness of our counterparts.

Finally, he also gets into the corresponding situation with his basic attitude.

Coming down and relaxing again is the order of the day when we have come back to the tough, difficult, and long-winded situations with our child.

Very few children enjoy school, even if their environment would be different.

I know from experience that even first-graders do not want to go to school at all once they have checked that they really have to go there every day.

If there are still caustic teachers, intrusive, rude, or even evil classmates, then as a mother and father you already have a hard time.

And then there are these tons of homework. You are already beating your ears hour after hour, a crying, tired child at the table.

Outside, the sun is shining, and few now decide to simply let the tasks be and go out with the child.

This would be clearly a better option.

Unfortunately, all the scrap in our head comes into play here again.

> what would the others say when my child goes to play instead of learning?
>
> how do I stand at school?
>
> what do the teachers say and think about me
>
> nothing becomes of the child if he does not learn from the beginning, tightand and neatly.

Oh ever, Oh ever. Do they already notice it? How hard it is to make life because of your environment. To howl.

Not only for the child, who in this way takes the fun of learning, school and childhood as a whole.

Now I remind them again of the sentence they said before I said about their cocky child:

"oh man, I've told you a thousand times, you never become anything because you're just too messy and lazy."

Do you realise what I have just said, how many times have I said that?

How would I feel as a child, how does my child feel?

The best way to cover up this negative sentence is to replace it with a positive sentence.

Or you try to cover it up in the hope that the darling has not heard this. But you are often mistaken. Children hear more than you know and often hear exactly what they should not hear.

I have 4 children; I know exactly what I am talking about.

If you want to think negatively, to formulate positively, you usually try to do so.

It no longer says, "You will never become anything because you are so messy."

but: "Tough, you will make it. You can do it, I know you can keep order."

This is a good start. It would be particularly good if you really believe what you are saying. Children are also aware of this very well.

As an adult, of course, you can say these affirmations repeatedly, yourself or to the child, until you believe it yourself.

Unfortunately, this is again difficult. Because now we have not only the 1000 times say thing, but also our brain, which simply wants to live in peace and tranquility. leben möchte.

We don't use our brains completely anyway. And a lot of things are going on, as we know ourselves in "Autopilot". Let us think of breathing, blood circulation and all other bodily functions.

Spiritually, our brain feels extremely comfortable when everything is done in an orderly fashion.

As soon as something unforeseen happens, the alarm goes off.

This alarm always expresses itself negatively in the case of negative thoughts. We get sweats, the pulse goes up, we get puter-red with anger, we race out, scream around, throw objects around the area and especially nasty contemporaries, unfortunately to many parents, shout at their children and use physical violence.

Hardly anyone is immune from it.

Why? Because we feel shaken in our foundations when something doesn't go the way we would like it to.

In the case of children, it is often the case that we want the best, but the way to it is pretty much the most stupid we have chosen.

As our brains, we need to teach that change can be a good thing. Nowadays we rarely die when we sleep outside, for example, which could be a disaster for the bear hunter in the cave thousands of years ago.

For the most part, however, the programs in our brains have not changed. It's about getting through life well and safely.

So let your brain notice and learn that the change to the positive is really positive!

If it triggers an alarm that we can't stop despite playing through a situation before, then try to come down again. The brain reacts to ATMEN quite quickly.

inhale - exhale

inhale - exhale

again, and again.

Drink a glass of water and become aware. Everything that happens is not up to you. It is important to realize that almost everything takes placein the mind due to the wrongprogramming.

inhale - exhale.

Light a candle with your child. Marvel at the light.

- goes out for a walk. Cook a cocoa.

Hug yourself!!!

Apologize to yourself and forgive yourself!

You arrive inside when you realize you can change!

Do not let the wave of your negative emotions carry you away. It is not worth it. Nobody wants you to do anything bad. Especially not your child!

It cannot help it either. It already has the same programs in mind as you.

Sit down and paint/ draw. Draw your life.

Draw your feelings. And i'll know what you're thinking.

How much of it are YOU? How much of it you've been told that this is supposed to be you, but it's what others want to live, want to do.

Remember who wants to change you, just don't want to change yourself.

But it also works with writing down, painting, making a collage out of it and looking and reading again and again.

A collage hereby means to illustrate its goals.

What happens when I'm a better person, take more and better care of myself and my family. I care less about my environment, but finally realize myself.

How much better will it be for me and my children, my partner, etc.?

Suddenly the hopes and desires and goals

and visions that had already been buried.

It is also much easier to program your brain on something you have in front of you!

Especially creative minds can alsozu create a mind map there. Which can be expanded again and again.

As often as possible, but the best way to spend a day on each belief is to transform the next belief.

There are no rules for this. Everyone needs to know and know the different ways and find the right way for themselves.

Many people use multiple methods at the same time.

We must not forget that it has taken years for negative thoughts to become established, that it could take longer to replace them with positive ones.

Practice also makes the master here. It also brings truly little constant pressure to put itself under pressure, that something absolutely has to change immediately, this only makes our brain audible if not an alarm threatens soon.

In the end, for each of us, who eats attentively and consciously at his behavior, feelings, words and actions. He realizes at some point WHAT drives him.

What are the real reasons for his behavior? And how he can behave differently in the future. Positive.

Let us do this as often as possible. Watching a bit from the outside and consciously reflecting on our behaviour.

This has already taken more than the first step towards a positive change in his life!

Anyone who hears his inner voice again, trusts his gut feeling and pays attention to the inner observer is already extremely far in the awareness of himself.

Always remember it!

You are the Creator of Your Life.

You create your everyday life yourself.

God is in you and in everything around you.

The angels accompany and protect you.

We are all on earth to grow.

The engine of our actions should be love.

We create our own paradise.

Hell is also in us, but we can keep it small.

As in the inside - so on the outside.

Trust in you.

Trust your heart, it beat even before you could even think.

Listen to your inner voice.

You can do anything.

You are part of the big picture.

You are not alone in the universe.

Everything is in harmony with you.

You are the creator of your reality and the reality of your children.

think wise

First think and then talk, you do not do anything wrong with that.

If you do not have anything positive to say, leave it.

Think about your behavior every day.

The others cannot do anything for your behavior.

Everyone reflects theiresurroundings.

Always be upright and believe in the good.

Be a role model for others and yourself.

Have confidence.

Trust your inner child.

Listen to your inner observer.

Recognize love and be not afraid of it.

Love is for everyone.

There is enough for everyone. No matter what.

You are a child of God and God loves you.

You are protected and loved.

Peace comes from within.

Love and happiness can be shared indefinitely.

Be cheerful.

Be grateful.

Life is a gift. Keep it good.

Trust and love are the key to happiness.

Everything will be fine.

Every human being is valuable.

Every human being is precious.

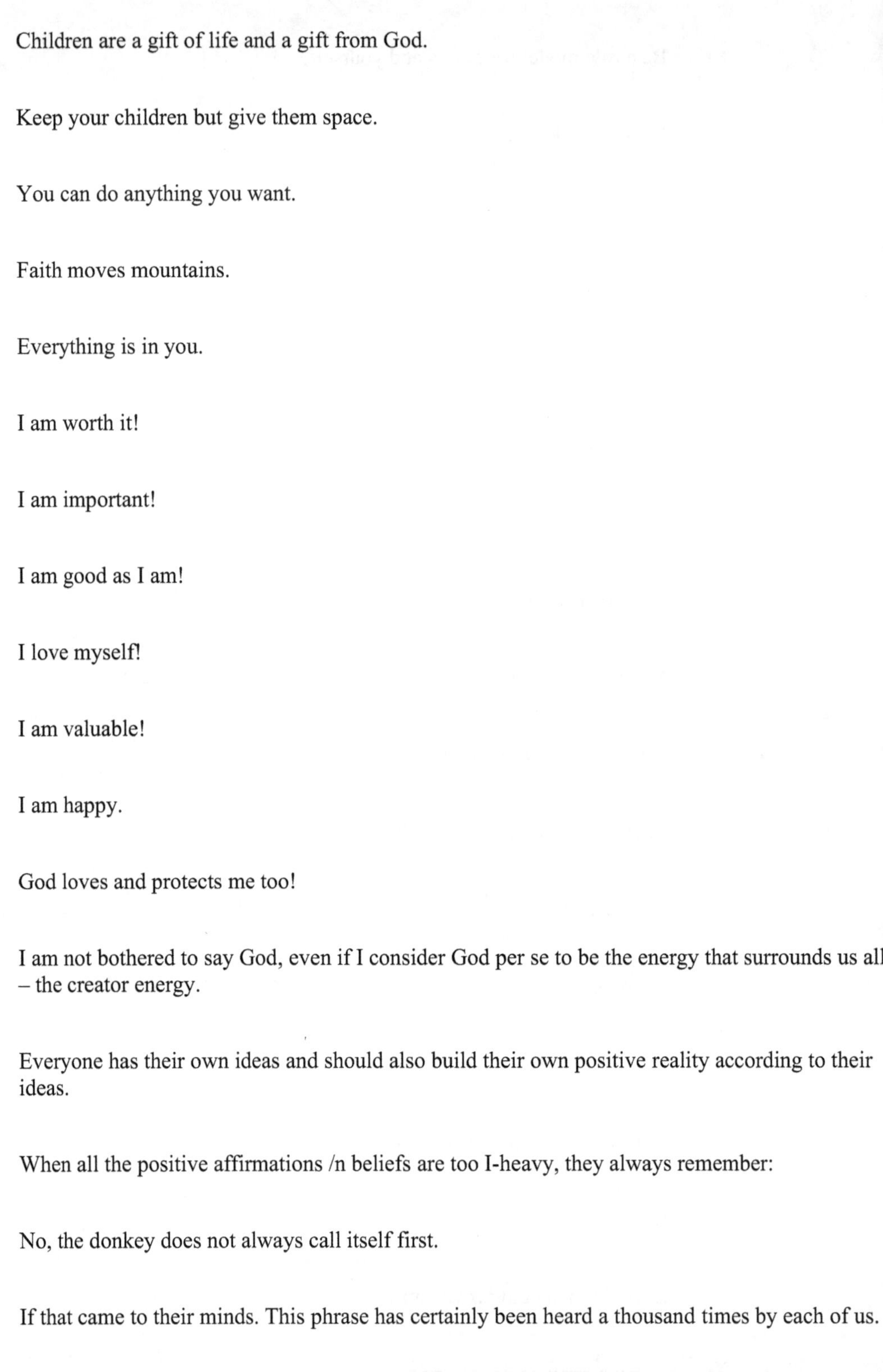

Children are a gift of life and a gift from God.

Keep your children but give them space.

You can do anything you want.

Faith moves mountains.

Everything is in you.

I am worth it!

I am important!

I am good as I am!

I love myself!

I am valuable!

I am happy.

God loves and protects me too!

I am not bothered to say God, even if I consider God per se to be the energy that surrounds us all – the creator energy.

Everyone has their own ideas and should also build their own positive reality according to their ideas.

When all the positive affirmations /n beliefs are too I-heavy, they always remember:

No, the donkey does not always call itself first.

If that came to their minds. This phrase has certainly been heard a thousand times by each of us.

How can you take good care of others if you do not love yourself?

We also need to teach ourselves and our children that one's own body is the most important thing you have. In addition to mind and heart.

And that includes starting with ourselves!

Joy

Today is a beautiful day.

I love my life and my life loves me.

I am happy.

In me it is bright.

All is well!

I am safe and secure.

Nothing can happen to me.

I think it is great that everyone is nice to me!

Courage

I am strong!

I can do it!

I can!

I can do whatever I want!

I am full of confidence.

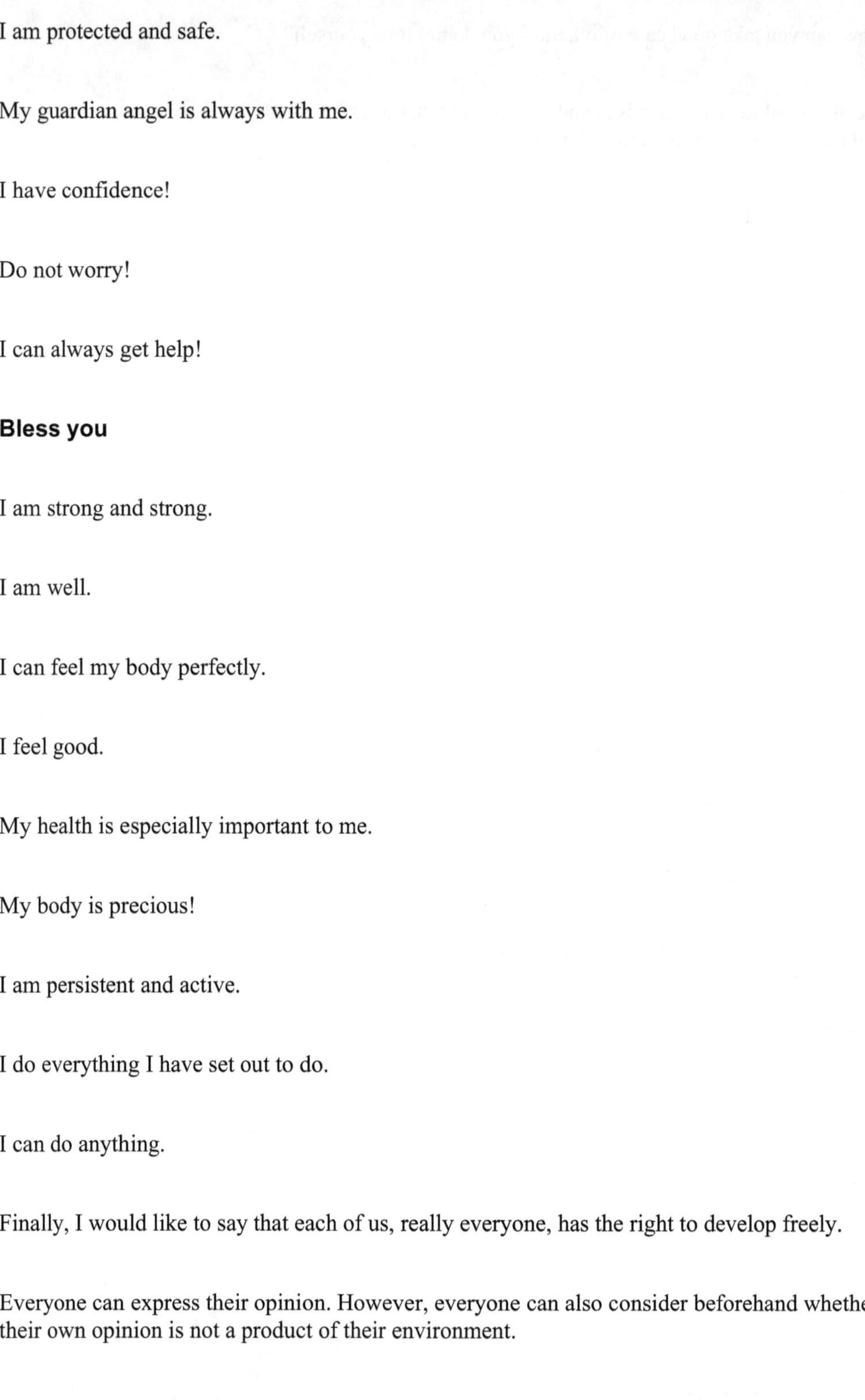

I am protected and safe.

My guardian angel is always with me.

I have confidence!

Do not worry!

I can always get help!

Bless you

I am strong and strong.

I am well.

I can feel my body perfectly.

I feel good.

My health is especially important to me.

My body is precious!

I am persistent and active.

I do everything I have set out to do.

I can do anything.

Finally, I would like to say that each of us, really everyone, has the right to develop freely.

Everyone can express their opinion. However, everyone can also consider beforehand whether their own opinion is not a product of their environment.

If this is the case, then form your own opinion. Do not rely blindly on others.

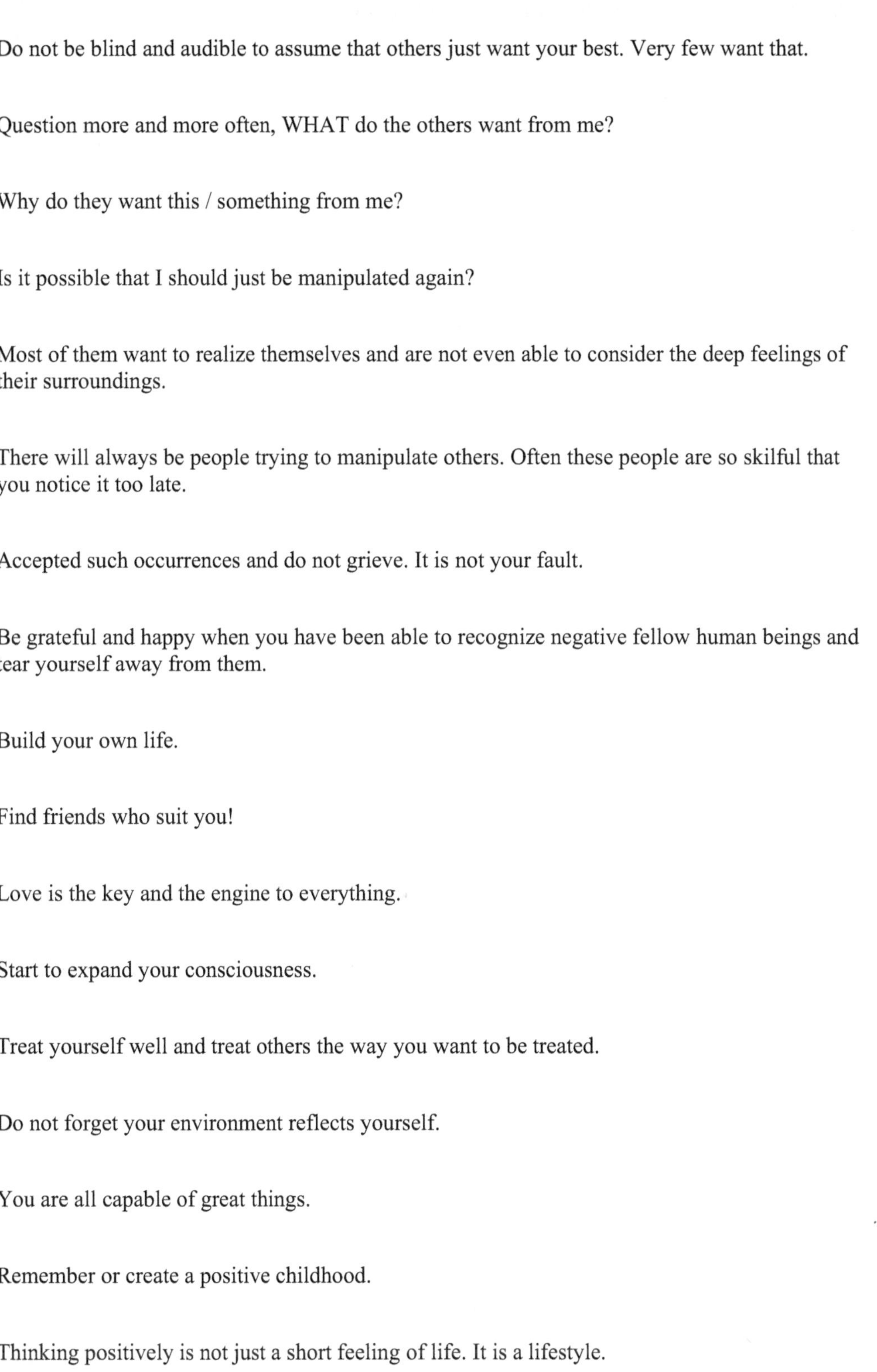

Do not be blind and audible to assume that others just want your best. Very few want that.

Question more and more often, WHAT do the others want from me?

Why do they want this / something from me?

Is it possible that I should just be manipulated again?

Most of them want to realize themselves and are not even able to consider the deep feelings of their surroundings.

There will always be people trying to manipulate others. Often these people are so skilful that you notice it too late.

Accepted such occurrences and do not grieve. It is not your fault.

Be grateful and happy when you have been able to recognize negative fellow human beings and tear yourself away from them.

Build your own life.

Find friends who suit you!

Love is the key and the engine to everything.

Start to expand your consciousness.

Treat yourself well and treat others the way you want to be treated.

Do not forget your environment reflects yourself.

You are all capable of great things.

Remember or create a positive childhood.

Thinking positively is not just a short feeling of life. It is a lifestyle.

Educate yourself. Do not lose the fun of education.

Only informed people are strong people.

Sheep run with the crowd. Are you sheep?

Dare to do the impossible - trust yourself. You make it.

Seek help, you think you need help.

Your inner voice will lead you to the right helper.

Rely on the first impression. Often that's the right idea.

Trust your intuition!

Don't listen to each other's stupid talk!

You are your own Creator.

Everyone has the right to be free and happy. Each!

I wish each one of you a beautiful life. Full of happiness, wonder and satisfaction. Beyond war, hunger, hardship, and misery.

Find yourself.

Familiar!

Trust in yourself, on your intuition, on your gut feeling.

On love and life.

www.ingramcontent.com/pod-product-compliance
Lightning Source LLC
LaVergne TN
LVHW010514160826
845677LV00012B/2857